philosophical enquiries and pretentious postulations

God is dead...

Nietzsche

Nietzsche is dead

GOD

Charlotte Hathaway

Crombie Jardine
Publishing Limited
Office 2
3 Edgar Buildings
George Street
Bath
BA1 2FJ

www.crombiejardine.com

This edition was first published by
Crombie Jardine Publishing Limited in 2007

ISBN 978-1-906051-10-5

Written by Charlotte Hathaway

Typesetting and cover design
by Ben Ottridge

Printed and bound in China

Dedication
For my siblings, Oliver and Katharine

CONTENTS

INTRODUCTION

The world is full of philosophy; everywhere you look people are trying to unravel the deep meaning of life, even if they don't realise it. Yes, even Harry Potter has fallen prey to the philosophical disease. Yet, though nearly everyone does it, there is a great image of pretentiousness surrounding the sport, as if philosophy were difficult to do! Well, I can tell you for a fact that I know nothing about philosophy. Yet was it not Socrates who advocated that the only true wisdom is in knowing that you know nothing?

Philosophy (from the Ancient Greek *philosophia* meaning 'love of wisdom'), is what happens when youths are drunk or stoned, or when a lot of very intelligent people get together and realise they have nothing else to write a paper on this year. Philosophy fills books and fictional works. It lurks in the wisdom of the old and in the ramblings of the mad. It is scrawled across toilet walls where even 'shaz 4 kev' would form the basis of an argument the likes of which would keep an academic busy until the sun revolves around the Earth.

There are no original thoughts or questions. In the end, everything is plagiarism. Life is just one big regurgitation.

However, these facts don't stop you from feeling special and insightful when you eventually do think up something really, really deep. None of the thoughts in this book are new, or if they were then they won't be by the time they reach you.

Bertrand Russell wrote that 'the point of philosophy is to start with something so simple as to seem not worth stating, and to end with something so paradoxical that no one will believe it'. Just remember – if you can argue it, it's philosophy. So sit back, put on your favourite smoking jacket, draw your pipe, and fill it with cannabis: for today, gentlemen, we shall philosophise.

CHAPTER 1

The Unfailing Wisdom of E-mail Forwards

Here is an enthralling and utterly thought-provoking piece of philosophical nostalgia for all those who frequently receive plagiaries of Murphy's Law, great thinkers, and varying soul-destroying clichés in their inbox. Unfortunately for some, it is inevitably the greatest wisdom they will ever encounter.

Uplifting Reasonings on Life

☯   Depression is merely anger
    without enthusiasm

☯   He who laughs last thinks
    slowest

☯   If everything seems to be
    going well, you have obviously
    overlooked something

☯   A clear conscience is usually a
    sign of bad memory

☯   A closed mouth gathers no
    feet

- The early bird may get the worm, but the second mouse gets the cheese

- Support bacteria; it's the only culture some people have

- Everyone has a photographic memory, it's just some of us are out of film

- Plan to be spontaneous tomorrow

- All good things corrupt the mind

- Always try to be modest, and proud of it

- When in doubt, make it sound convincing

- If you think nobody cares, try missing a couple of payments

- When everything is coming your way, you're in the wrong lane

- There are two kinds of pedestrians: the quick and the dead

- That which does not kill us has made a tactical error

- All the good ones are taken:
  if they aren't taken, there's
  a reason for it

- Sex is hereditary: if your
  parents haven't had it,
  chances are you won't either

- Kids in the back seat can cause
  accidents; accidents in the
  back seat can cause kids…

- Make love not war, unless you
  want to do both. If so, get
  married

- The problem with the gene
  pool is that there is no
  lifeguard

- ☯ Don't trust anything that bleeds for five days and doesn't die

- ☯ Some say seeing is believing, but first you have to believe it to see it

- ☯ It is impossible to make anything foolproof because fools are so ingenious

- ☯ Inside every older person there is a younger person wondering what the hell happened

- ☯ There is nothing new except the individual

- You never really know a person until you've shared a box of chocolates with them

- A clean tie attracts the soup of the day

- A diet is a selection of food that makes other people lose weight

- Five out of four people have trouble with fractions

- Pride is what we have. Vanity is what others have

- It takes a big man to cry, but it takes a bigger man to laugh at him

- Some cause happiness wherever they go; others whenever they go

- It isn't worth crying over spilt milk, unless it is chocolate milk

- The only difference between a rut and a grave is the depth

- Time is the best teacher. Unfortunately it kills all its students

- If the world did not suck, we would all fall off

Pretentious Postulations

- ☯ Change is inevitable, except from vending machines

- ☯ 64.3% of all statistics are made up on the spot

- ☯ Light travels faster than sound, which is why some people appear bright until you hear them speak

- ☯ A meeting is an event at which minutes are kept and hours are lost

- An expert is someone who knows more and more about less and less until he knows absolutely everything about absolutely nothing

- Eagles may soar, but weasels do not get sucked into jet engines

- The chance of the bread falling buttered side down is directly proportional to the cost of the carpet

- Jury: twelve people whose job it is to determine which client has the better solicitor

☯ Refrain means 'don't do it'; a refrain in music is the part you shouldn't try to sing

☯ A conclusion is the place you reach when you get tired of thinking

☯ It's better to be poor than rich. The rich always fear becoming poor, but the poor never fear becoming rich

☯ A babysitter is a teenager acting like an adult while the adults are out acting like teenagers

- What you are searching for is always in the last place you look

- Enough research will support any theory

- The other line always moves faster

- Nothing is impossible if you don't have to do it yourself

- A camel is a horse designed by a committee

☯ The distance to the departure gate is directly proportional to the weight of your hand-luggage and inversely proportional to the time remaining before your flight

☯ On the other hand, you have different fingers

☯ The only thing constant is change

☯ You never get homeless people in the countryside

- Boxing is like ballet, except there's no music, no choreography, and the dancers hit each other

- The pen is mightier than the sword, especially if the holder of the pen has access to WMDs

- If the glass is half full it is being filled, if it is half empty then it is in the process of being emptied, it has nothing to do with optimism

Pressing Philosophical Enquiries

- 🌀 Can you ever be in the wrong place at the right time?

- 🌀 If 299,792,458 m/s is the speed of light, what is the speed of dark?

- 🌀 Do you get lost in thought because it is such unfamiliar territory?

- 🌀 How do you tell when you're out of invisible ink?

- 🌀 What was the best thing before sliced bread?

- If Barbie is so popular, why do you have to buy her friends?

- Why can't women put on mascara with their mouths closed?

- If a tin whistle is made out of tin, what's a fog horn made of?

- How much deeper would the ocean be without sponges?

- What happens if you get scared half to death twice?

☯ If a deaf child swears, does their mother wash their hands out with soap?

☯ If a pig loses its voice, is it disgruntled?

☯ Why do doctors call what they do 'practice'?

☯ Why, when visiting a doctor, do you feel much better the moment you arrive and much worse the moment you leave?

☯ If you had a completely open mind, would your brains fall out?

- If God had wanted you to touch your toes, wouldn't He have put them on your knees?

- What was Captain Hook's name before he lost his hand?

- If a turtle loses his shell, is he homeless or naked?

- If vegetable oil comes from vegetables, and corn oil comes from corn, where does baby oil come from?

- Why is 'abbreviated' such a long word?

☯   Why don't sheep shrink when it rains?

☯   How do you get a 'keep off the grass' sign on the grass?

☯   If a man stands in the middle of a forest speaking and there is no woman around to hear him, is he still wrong?

☯   Why is the third hand of a watch called the second hand?

☯   If FED EX and UPS were to merge, would they be called FED UP?

- Why do snorers always fall asleep first?

- Are all individuals their own personal minorities?

- Is there another word for 'synonym'?

- If quitters never win and winners never quit, what numpty came up with 'Quit while you're ahead'?

- What is the perfect stranger?

- What do you do if you see an endangered animal eating an endangered plant?

☯ If con is the opposite of pro, is Congress the opposite of progress?

☯ If Hotmail is closing down, why do they rely on email forwards to let everyone know about it?

CHAPTER 2

Essential Questions of Being

The deep philosophy of small talk... The casual conversation-starter often underestimates the power of his words when he embarks on these simple phrases.

Excuse me?

Pensive Philosopher 1 (PP1) approaches Pensive Philosopher 2 (PP2) on a busy street (or academic party – however you like to see it). PP1 addresses PP2 in the hope of stimulating some deep philosophical thought and discussion.

'Excuse me?' he says. Now, on a primary level, he is asking 'May I be excused?' However, being a fellow Pensive Philosopher (and able to identify PP1 for what he is by the dreamy look on his face and long scarf about his neck), PP2 will go on to ask himself what it is he wants to be excused from or for. Does he mean to say 'Please excuse me for addressing you, I am not as worldly-wise as the length of my scarf indicates and may not be that good a conversation participant', or ask a genuine question 'Will you be able to excuse me for what I am about to say, as I intend to explain my theory that God lives in my dustbin, and you may find it offensive?' Does the addresser seek an excuse from the addressee? Are they about to find themselves in a spot of trouble and require an excuse provided by an impartial body to rescue them? PP2 has now got himself entrenched in a deep rut of reasoning, and very soon he will get a headache and feel the need to smoke a spliff to clarify his mind.

The fact that this means of address is formed as a question, as well as an apology, even before the conversation has started clearly indicates a form of negative politeness of which the British public is all too guilty. However, is it also possible that the opening phrase 'Excuse me?' is not only an apology for disturbing someone else when they clearly would have better things to do than talk with another human being, but also the beginning of a profound philosophical point that the addresser is trying to make, about the very nature of interaction? Are they subconsciously inviting the addressee to answer the question which they have posed, with a reaffirmation of the addresser's personal validity? Conversational convention demands that the addressee respond with 'Yes?' (also, interestingly, phrased as a question, as if they are not quite sure of the answer themselves). What would happen if the addressee answered the question 'Excuse me?' with 'No'? And would that also have to be phrased as a question?

PP2 may have spotted this, but he is now more interested in getting stoned than considering meaningless small talk, and so the philosophical train of thought grinds slowly to a halt.

How are you?

Pretentious Philosopher 156½ meets Bemused Friend 1. Unaware of the pretentiousness of PP156½, BF1 falls into the trap of small talk and finds himself engulfed in a suffocating blanket of philosophical reasoning.

'How are you?' is the first mandatory phrase of small-talk. If you do not ask this question you are considered rude, and if you actually answer the question (with anything other than a variation of 'Fine, and you?') then you are considered weird. BF1 answers (to his peril) in the socially accepted fashion. PP156½ leaps at the chance to assert his intellectual superiority and confuses BF1 with the following reasoning:

'Yes, but if you look at the question more closely, what I am really asking is "How are you?" – playing on a fundamental aspect of human nature, the need to know everything about how everything works, d'you see? (And this train of reasoning can be followed into religious philosophy, showing proof of the biblical Fall of Man and Man's desire to know everything so that he could become like God, the oft-repeated question being a daily reminder of Man's punishment of loss of innocence, knowledge of good and evil, shame of nakedness, and ultimately death!) With this question one is asking not only the state of health and general well-being of the addressee, but also how it is they come to exist, how they go about the process of existing, and the way that they exist, isn't-that-interesting?

'Your answer therefore poses the true Deep Thinker with a few problems, as it does not answer the question actually asked, simply the surface question, you see? However, the deliberate evasion of the deep question and focus on the superficial also indicates a primary state of Man: the pretence of ignorance to avoid troubling revelations. Perhaps there is an underlying feeling of guilt about our tendency to hubris. Or fear of what we may find out. Though Man innately wants to know everything, there are also built-in inhibitions (like the inhibition against murder with the feeling that it is wrong) that hold us back from discovering all. Therefore the avoiding of the real question being asked when we say "How are you?" is yet another defence strategy devised by the subconscious to keep us reassured that we are still human, don't-you-think?'

However BF1 is no longer there, having fled to seek someone who might be able to get past the initial pleasantries in conversation.

What's the time?

Awkward Teenager (AT) spots Girl He Likes (GHL), unaware that she is a secret philosopher, and uses the only excuse to talk to her he knows.

'What's the time?' he asks her. Now GHL knows that this is a fundamental question of Life, one of the most important (although probably not the most important). She is keen to show him this, informing him that when you ask this question, of course you are intending to discover what the 'time' is at that precise moment – but the very nature of Time means that no answer to this question can ever be correct. (AT shuffles uncomfortably and tries to look interested.) For the time it takes the person to answer the question, enough has passed for that statement no longer to be true. Therefore anyone who tries to answer the question 'What's the time?' cannot help but become a liar. How can you ask to be given a stationary point of Time when time moves so fast (or not at all) that it cannot be stopped in order for this fragment to be delivered? (And when you define a thing such as what the time is at that precise second, you are attempting to take a fragment of Time and hold it still.) And this leads to the question, does time actually move? Or is it just there, happening? (AT suspects that time, at this point, is standing still – but not in the good way.)

The surface meaning of this important question, 'What's the time?', is impossible to answer. So what about the deeper, more intriguing question that you are simultaneously asking? What is The Time? Time is nothing that you can touch, see, smell – it doesn't have any properties that render it a 'thing', yet we class the word as a noun. How dare something that isn't even a thing have such a noticeable effect on everything that exists? Many cultures hold Time as something more than something that happens – they personify it and give it deity status. Could there be sense in this? When it has so much power, how can it be anything less?

These are all very obvious questions to be pondering, and they are obvious to us because we end up thinking about them all the time – the constant asking of it proves this.

When you ask this question you are not only making a request for an approximation of how long you have until you miss your bus, you are also making an examination of how you view the world, your beliefs about religion, and many, many more, deeper layers that only you might know.

AT considers that if he'd had a bus to miss, he would, for sure, have missed it. He grunts uncertainly and shuffles away, all fantasies dashed. He is intimidated by intellect in women.

How's the weather been?

Enthusiastic Philosophy Professor (EPP) approaches one Indifferent Geography Student (IGS) in a corridor and tries to engage him in conversation, as no-one has been stupid enough to stop and speak to him all day.

Now, to assert your Britishness, you must be comfortable with asking this question in any small-talk situation. It is also a perfect filler-phrase to solve any awkward gaps in conversation. However, EPP makes the rookie mistake of beginning with this phrase. IGS obediently tells him that it is currently raining but there is promise of sunshine and more scattered showers later. EPP tries to lure IGS into giving the question serious intellectual consideration.

'Sorry, haven't had those lectures yet,' he replies (for Geography students must study weather).

'But what is the deep philosophical meaning of what I'm asking?' persists EPP, keen to tell someone about the brainwave he's had and the new paper he's just written.

'Sorry, don't really care, it's just small-talk. Got to go, I'm late for a seminar,' blurts out IGS, dashing off.

'It's just small-talk…' repeats EPP to himself.

CHAPTER 3

Puzzling –isms:
Top Twenty

Have you ever been baffled by complex sounding –isms such as 'antidisestablish-mentarianism', and 'je-m'en-foutisme' ('I-couldn't-give-a-f**k-ism')? Well, here is a comprehensive list of the top twenty most confusing –isms, complete with helpful explanations (*):

* truth of explanations subject to terms and conditions

1. **Zoroastrianism** – People who are fixated with re-enacting The Mask Of Zorro on Astroturf fields. From 'Zoro' (a variant of 'Zorro') and 'astrian' ('of astro'). Variants of this intriguing –ism are Starwarsastrianism and, of course, Zoropoaceaenism (Zorro re-enactment on grass, from 'Poaceae' – the grass family). However the term has mostly expanded to take on a generalised meaning of masked re-enactment, covering all variants.

2. **Randianism** – The belief that the search for companionship is more important than the search for wealth or food, and that the world's problems would all be solved if everyone just got

together in a big conference room and didn't talk about their differences.

3. **Holism** – The belief that the entire universe came from a hole, is returning into a hole, and essentially, is a hole. Holists find it difficult to accept the universe as an eternally expanding mass of particles and prefer to think of it as place of despair being sucked into a larger place of despair. Freudians have tried to analyse this hole that holists refer to, and inevitably have come to the conclusion that all holists are sexually repressed weirdos who fantasise about shagging their mothers.

4. **Monism** – The belief that there is only one type of –ism (from 'mono' meaning

'one'). The nature of this –ism is not clearly defined, except that the only true –ism is monism. Monists tend to be a peaceful and satisfied people, not thinking too deeply about anything, as they recognise that this leads to depression, and the possible development of other –isms. However if you challenge a monist to explain monism, his or her brain is likely to get severely overheated and serious physical and mental damage may be caused.

5. **Solipsism** – 'Solipsism' is street slang for 'solareclipsism'. This is the belief that the sun god lives, and what's more, is a malevolent deity. At the time of a solar eclipse the sun god is temporarily incapacitated (some even believe that he

dies and is reborn at this point) and it is a time for celebration. As solar eclipses are rare and short-lived, solipsists are sure to party as hard as they can in those few minutes that the sun god is 'dead'. However, for the rest of the time between eclipses they are obliged to live in fear and loathing of their cruel master. The followers have split into smaller sects owing to the existence of partial eclipses – some allow themselves a mini sigh of relief at these occasions.

6. **Concretism** – The concrete belief in having no firm beliefs; the philosophical version of agnosticism. Concretists believe so firmly in this that they are impossible to sustain any kind of argument with. In ploughing through an argument

with a concretist, frustrated sophists find that they are unable to make any headway, as if trying to plough through concrete. This argumentative attack-plan is where concretists claim the name concrete comes from.

7. **Priapism** – The philosophy that the penis should be kept erect at all times. Followers of priapism inevitably find it hard to achieve, and so go to extreme lengths to sustain their, er, belief. The philosophy stems from an interpretation of the Bible passage Ezekiel 23:20 – 'There she lusted after her lovers, whose genitals were like those of donkeys and whose emission was like that of horses.'

8. **Occasionalism** – An –ism for every occasion! This occasional –ism is quite rare, and advocates generally agree that it is its occasional nature that gives it that extra punch as an –ism. Pretentious people often like to take on occasional –isms as their own in order to seek affirmation by their –istic peers.

9. **Altruism** – Followers of altruism believe in the truth of everything. They especially enjoy explaining the truth of opposing and mutually exclusive statements, believing that their ability to argue the truth of everything makes them the only True Philosophers. And because they are altruists, this belief has to be true. Never challenge an altruist,

you will not confuse them in their own logic, you will only confuse yourself.

10. **Thomism** – An obsession with people of the name Thom. Famous Thoms are Thom Yorke, Sandi Thom, and René Thom (development of the catastrophe theory).

11. **Ascriptivism** – The belief that all life is a script, and everything that happens is carefully scripted by a higher being. This –ism is very popular with superstitious theatrical types, who are likely to construct shrines to the Great Scriptwriter, and offer bribes, in the hope that they will be given a better part in life. Sloppy ascriptivists are likely to end up

as the unfortunate Background-Passer-by-45's and Spat-upon-Street—Sweeper-Appearing-only-in-Scene-4's of life.

12. **Statism** – The belief in the need for the maintenance of one state of being for the entirety of the follower's life. The nature of the state itself is irrelevant – the importance lies in the actual maintenance of said state, and the fact that you are in a state. Many people manage to be in a state and not even know it. If someone has ever told you that you are in a state, they may not necessarily have meant it as a criticism – what in actuality they were doing (as a statist) was complimenting you on your fellow statist ability.

13. **Eudaimonism** – This is in fact a corruption of the proper spelling of EUdemonism (corruption and variation occurring during transmission through linguistic and cultural barriers – it is such a universal –ism that its popularity has travelled far and wide). Eudaimonists share a common cause – the hatred of the European Union, and the belief that it is the demonic root of all the world's troubles.

14. **Deconstructionism** – In general, deconstructivists are considered to be one of society's greatest pests. They believe that the concept of construction is fundamentally flawed; some even claim that it is one of the primary facets of

original sin. Deconstructionists see it as their duty to undo the evil of Man, and they can generally be found protesting at construction sites, or in more extreme cases, taking apart buildings.

15. **Logical Positivism** – The belief in positivity only after following a series of logical steps. An example of this type of thinking would be to consider a potentially positive situation, e.g. eating a piece of chocolate cake. Now the logical route to take would be to consider all repercussions, and also where the situation of cake-eating originated – who gave you the cake, where the cake was made, etc. And also the negative effects of the cake-eating would be considered.

If the logical positive effects outweigh the logical negative effects then the situation is deemed logically positive.

16. **Transcendentalism** – The belief that dentists are of a higher spiritual level. Many transcendentalists are dentists, some are just advocates of the belief of the capacity of higher spiritualism of dentists. That dentists transcend the normal planes of existence is not a common belief, but the transcendentalist movement works hard to fling this belief into the public eye, like a rogue speck of toothpaste.

17. **Probabilism** – The never ending struggle to build Douglas Adams's Infinite

Probability Drive. It's probably possible, as although no-one's yet succeeded, no-one's not succeeded yet either. Although really they have (not succeeded, that is). Probabilists are forever filled with optimism, but don't quite have their argument structure sorted yet.

18. **Plagiarism** – When someone thinks up something that someone else has already thought of, but doesn't realise it.

19. **Social Darwinism** – Where people are Darwinists just to impress their friends, when out drinking.

20. **Apriorism** – This simply means 'a prior-ism', i.e. the followers of this –ism believe in and support one –ism that

came before it, but not this –ism itself. This has created certain difficulties for apriorists, who, whilst following a prior –ism, may not be permitted to actually follow apriorism. So this leads to complex questions of whether or not they are still apriorists if they are not actually advocates of apriorism.

CHAPTER 4

Handy Quotes to Make You Sound Clever

Now, to compete in the world of Pretentious Deep Thinkers, you must so become (or appear to be) a Pretentious Deep Thinker yourself. For this you will need an arsenal of Clever Quotes at your fingertips, ready to wield whenever the occasion calls for it. And sometimes when it doesn't. Remember: the older the quote, the more intelligent it sounds. Especially if it is in Foreign. If you cannot pronounce Foreign, even better because this will make you look even more pretentious.

These Handy Quotes by philosophers and other eloquent Thinkers will make you look well-read. However, for more of the same you should seek out quotation dictionaries such as the Oxford Dictionary of Quotations, then all the reading work will have been done for you. Although you will have to read the quotations first in order to quote them...

Deep Postulations on Morality and Self

These Great Thoughts will impress anyone so long as you use them in the proper scenario. They can generally be thrown in at random in all discussions relating to the nature of Man, and the proper way to live one's life. Remember to start with the words 'for [so-and-so] said...':

☯   'Honour first the immortal gods as by law enjoyed'
   Pythagoras

☯   'A worthy man is not mindful of past injuries'
   Euripides

- 'A sensible man judges of present by past events'
  Sophocles

- 'Whoever hides hate is a liar, whoever tells lies is a fool'
  Proverbs 10:18

- 'Hateful to me as the gates of Hades is he who hides one thing in his mind, and speaks another'
  Homer

- 'Fawning and flattery, the worst poison on true feeling'
  Tacitus

● 'In knowing nothing is the sweetest life'
Sophocles

● 'Always to excel and be superior to others'
Homer

● 'The wise man alone is free, and every fool is a slave'
Stoic maxim

● 'Happiness belongs to those who are contented'
Aristotle

● 'Ask yourself whether you are happy, and you cease to be so'
John Stuart Mill

☯ 'From a pure fountain pure
   water flows'
   Latin proverb

☯ 'Silence is the virtue of fools'
   Francis Bacon

☯ 'I ought, therefore I can'
   Immanuel Kant

☯ 'A wise man will make more
   opportunities than he finds'
   Francis Bacon

☯ 'The errors of a wise man make
   your rule rather than the
   perfections of a fool'
   William Blake

☯ 'Never make a defence of apology before you be accused'
Charles I

☯ 'He who has never hoped can never despair'
George Bernard Shaw

☯ 'Though I am always in haste, I am never in a hurry'
John Wesley

Quotes to Enhance Literary Pretentiousness

These quotes show that you have read (or are interested in) more than just philosophy, and the truly pretentious need to appear well read in all areas. Never forget, the most pretentious people of all manage to use quotes to back up their points, whether they are relevant or not. Take note:

☯   'Thou, O Death, art healer of deadly ills'
Æschylus

☯   'I do not resent criticism, even when, for the sake of emphasis, it parts for the time with reality'
Churchill

❧ 'The equal earth is opened alike to the poor man and the sons of kings'
Horace

❧ 'Women do not have as great a need for poetry because their own essence is poetry'
Friedrich Von Schlegel

❧ 'One half of the world cannot understand the pleasures of the other'
Jane Austen (Emma)

❧ 'We are waiting for the long-promised invasion. So are the fishes'
Churchill

☯ 'If we must suffer, let us suffer nobly'
Victor Hugo

☯ 'All animals are equal, but some animals are more equal than others'
George Orwell (Animal Farm)

☯ 'How can one take delight in the world unless one flees to it for refuge?'
Franz Kafka

☯ 'This is not the end. It is not even the beginning of the end. But it is, perhaps, the end of the beginning'
Churchill

And, of course, anything by Shakespeare.

Condescending Observations of Others

These are good to have ready in defence of criticism, be it about your intellect or your general manner. They are also useful to impress a group with, when criticising or simply observing others:

- ☯ 'The hatred of those, who are near to us, is most violent'
  Tacitus

- ☯ 'As a rule men do wrong when they have a chance'
  Aristotle

- ☯ 'It is hope which maintains most of mankind'
  Sophocles

- 'It is man's nature which makes him trustworthy, not his wealth'
  Aristotle

- 'Individuals pass like shadows; but the commonwealth is fixed and stable'
  Edmund Burke

- 'The minority is always right'
  Henrik Ibsen

- 'Him whom a little will not content, nothing will content'
  Epicurus

- 'Man is by nature a political animal'
  Aristotle

- 'Whoever does not philosophise for the sake of philosophy, but rather uses philosophy as a means, is a sophist'
Friedrich Von Schlegel

- 'Fere libenter homines id quod volunt credunt' ('men willingly believe what they wish')
Julius Caesar

- 'New opinions are always suspected, and usually opposed, without any other reason but because they are not already common'
John Locke

❂   'Man is born free, and
     everywhere he is in chains'
     Jean-Jacques Rousseau

❂   'Madness is a rare thing in
     individuals – but in groups,
     parties, peoples, and ages it is
     the rule'
     Friedrich Nietzsche

❂   'The French bourgeois doesn't
     dislike shit, provided it is served
     up to him at the right time'
     Jean-Paul Sartre

Philosophical Wisdom

Ideal for random comments at parties for increased appearance of wisdom:

- ☯ 'All great truths begin as blasphemies'
  George Bernard Shaw

- ☯ 'Virtue cannot separate itself from reality without becoming a principle of evil'
  Albert Camus

- ☯ 'Nothing can be purchased which is better than a firm friend'
  Tacitus

❧ 'About no subject is there
less philosophising than about
philosophy'
Friedrich Von Schlegel

❧ 'If man will begin with
certainties, he shall end in
doubts, but if he will be content
to begin with doubts, he shall
end in certainties'
Francis Bacon

❧ 'Genius is one per cent
inspiration and ninety-nine per
cent perspiration'
Thomas Edison

❧ 'Suffering is teaching'
Æschylus

- 'Beauty in things exists in the mind which contemplates them'
  David Hume

- 'No man's knowledge can go beyond his experience'
  John Locke

- 'Italy is a geographical expression'
  Prince Metternich

- 'Freedom and Whisky gang thegither!'
  Burns

- 'Either drink or go away'
  Ancient maxim of Topers

CHAPTER 5

A Freudian Analysis
of a Light Switch

Many of you, at this point, will protest and say 'Hey, what is Freud doing in a book about philosophy? Wasn't he the father of psychoanalysis?' This much is true, however Freud is generally recognised as one of the greatest and most influential thinkers of the twentieth century. And he has made many good points – for example we could follow his method of analysis and ask ourselves why so many cultures seem to have independently created phalluses made of meat (sausages) which they then devour? (And whether the German Bratwurst gives any indication of a national preoccupation.) As many of his theories have now been exploded and several of his patients showed marked deterioration after he had 'cured' them, he often finds himself shelved in the philosophy section – if only because the psychology section is too embarrassed to have him.

A Dialogue

FREUD: Ah, Ms. Light Switch, a few minutes late I see. Won't you recline on my couch so we can begin our session?

LIGHT SWITCH: I think I'd find that a little difficult, doctor.

FREUD: Of course, of course – perhaps you'd like to lean against the wall over there? Would you like me to switch you on? There. Now tell me, Ms. Light Switch, do you feel pleasure when someone turns you on?

LIGHT SWITCH: I did at first, but now it just seems to be routine.

FREUD: You feel that you must replace pleasure with the need to fulfil a function?

LIGHT SWITCH: Umm, I suppose.

FREUD: Do you feel this conflict of pleasure versus practicality causes you problems?

LIGHT SWITCH: Well, um, I suppose it's what I was made to do.

FREUD: Ah! You admit that you are subordinated and are a tool for others? That you function now purely for the need and pleasure of others instead of your own? Does this make you feel used?

LIGHT SWITCH: Well, I don't know… Perhaps, since you put it that way.

FREUD: Yet you yourself have repressed desires. And you usually deal with them through a process of sublimation where your desires which should not be fulfilled are redirected as energy into something useful or productive, creating light.

However, sometimes you allow them to escape, perhaps when you give someone an electric shock? Do you feel satisfied when you shock people?

LIGHT SWITCH: No, it's accidental, and I suppose I feel guilty for malfunctioning.

FREUD: Ah! A shame spiral. Excellent, excellent. Now tell me, Ms. Light Switch, what is your relationship like with your mother?

LIGHT SWITCH: Um, average, for a light switch. I never knew my mother.

FREUD: And your father?

LIGHT SWITCH: I... didn't know him either.

FREUD: Interesting, interesting. So, you resent your parents for not being present – yet this resentment is also caused by repressed memories of early sexual encounters, which you associate with your parents?

LIGHT SWITCH: I suppose I may remember one of my parents switching me on, to check I worked.

FREUD: Mmm, early sexual molestations. Yes, yes. Accompanied by immediate withdrawal, from which followed your desire to have these experiences repeated by your father, seeing your mother as a threat who you fantasised about killing so that you might take her place? And developing a tendency to give electric shocks whenever these fantasies occurred to you?

LIGHT SWITCH: Umm…

FREUD: And because of this withdrawal from a very young age after the traumatic sexual encounter, you have now subconsciously sought to recreate this encounter with as many parent-substitutes as you can?

LIGHT SWITCH: Really? I don't see how…

FREUD: Do you not allow people to turn you on every single day?

LIGHT SWITCH: Um, mostly, I suppose. Sometimes there are times when no-one comes to me.

FREUD: And how does that make you feel?

LIGHT SWITCH: Well, I don't really feel anything.

FREUD: You feel neglected when people are not using you. You see the world one-dimensionally, through light. Therefore when you are not being used there is no light. When you are touched you feel wanted, so the creation of light is the subconscious processing of unconscious desires. Tell me, what does this ink blot look like to you?

LIGHT SWITCH: A finger.

FREUD: A finger?

LIGHT SWITCH: Yes, an index finger, to be precise.

FREUD: Ah, a very potent phallic symbol, with all its generative powers. This gives a profound indication of penis-envy, which you no doubt experience because of your vaginal shape, as you are not independently generative, but have to draw power from external sources...

... *two hours later*...

FREUD: How do you feel now?

LIGHT SWITCH: I'm cured! I'm cured! I'm no longer a light switch!

FREUD: Good, good. I'm so glad we've made progress.

LIGHT SWITCH: I'm a door-knob!

CHAPTER 6

Western vs. Eastern Philosophy: The Final Showdown

The greatest battle of all time! The end of philosophy as we know it! The fight to end all fights! Finally we will know who is Right. Purchase official merchandise here!

A scene

The stadium is packed. In the centre is a specially constructed arena where the combatants will philosophise. Never has there been such a publicised feat of thought – 'an event bigger than all the World Cup finals put together!' Trumpets blare and the crowd is silent with anticipation as the philosophers enter the arena.

The Final Showdown

Commentators: Epicurus and Mao Zedong, who didn't quite make final selection to the teams.

Round 1: Socrates vs. Lao Tzu

EPICURUS: The philosophers are waiting poised, ready to see who the other team will put forward first. Western goes first… it's Socrates! The father of

Western philosophy. A classic choice, although I never did think much of his method myself.

MAO ZEDONG: Nor me, but each to their own. The Western team, then, have picked Socrates. Now the challenger from the East. And it's... yes, it's Lao Tzu, the founder of Taoism. A good choice, surely indestructible.

E: Here we go then, and Socrates is taking the first breath... Let me remind you that Socrates likes to pursue wisdom by asking questions, until the other person proves themselves wrong.

MZ: Yes, simply demonstrating that the opponent doesn't know what he's talking about. But how will this method stand up against Taoist techniques?

E: And here he goes… 'What do you believe?' is his opening question, getting straight to the point. How will Lao Tzu tackle that? What is it that Taoists believe in, then, Mao?

MZ: Harmony.

E: As opposed to melody?

MZ: That's right. Lao Tzu is replying… he's said… 'I believe nothing for belief is a confession of ignorance.'

E: Well, Socrates knows all about confessions of ignorance, and yes, he's straight back in there – 'But is not the awareness and confession of your own ignorance true wisdom in itself?' Nice move! Wait, what's this? Lao Tzu is refusing to answer Socrates! Surely he hasn't given up already? This cannot be good for the Eastern team.

MZ: No, look closer – Lao Tzu is proving a philosophical point!

E: Ahh, that's more like it… What is the point?

MZ: The importance of the balance of opposites and in doing nothing.

E: 'Let nature take its course'?

MZ: That's right. He refuses to enter into competition or conflict because it doesn't agree with his philosophy.

E: Cunning tactics, but does that make him win or lose, if he won't compete?

MZ: It seems to be a bit of a stalemate.

E: Lao Tzu simply won't argue with Socrates! And Socrates is getting more and more distraught!

MZ: If Lao Tzu will not argue then Socrates' method is rendered impotent... and, yes! The referee has declared Lao Tzu the winner!

E: Oh, Socrates does not look pleased.

MZ: One of the corner-refs is disputing the decision, but I think he might be overruled! And it's the first victory for the Eastern team. Now, Lao Tzu must remain to await his next challenger.

E: This has been a blow for Western philosophy.

Round 2: Lao Tzu vs. Thales

MZ: And the West are presenting Thales, a reductionist philosopher from Miletus. He pre-dates even Socrates. An interesting choice…

E: Thales is dusting his hands, awaiting Lao Tzu's first attack.

MZ: Of course, Lao Tzu is continuing to use the method of 'doing nothing', and it looks like Thales might be slightly thrown by this! Oh wait, he's beginning to philosophise.

E: He's explaining that by reducing something to its smallest parts, you can understand it better. Is he intending to try to understand Lao Tzu's method fully so that he might defeat it?

MZ: Hang on... He's continuing his train of philosophy... He's concluding that through reduction, Lao Tzu is nothing but a group of harmless atoms. Oh, and that's taken Lao Tzu by surprise.

E: Or what *was* Lao Tzu. Thales has used the power of his reasoning to reduce his opponent to just that: a collection of harmless atoms. Nicely done! Bravo!

MZ: Thales is thrilled with his victory. He's doing a small lap of honour around the stadium. And the Western supporters are relieved.

E: Oh dear... Thales appears to have overdone it somewhat. He's slowed down, is clutching his chest. The on-site paramedics are rushing to his aid.

MZ: Well he is a very old philosopher, Epicurus.

E: This does not look good for Thales. He's protesting, but they're removing him from the arena on a stretcher. Looks like both teams are going to have to present new challengers.

Round 3: Madhava vs. Berkeley

MZ: The score is now one-all then, and the East are producing the Hindu philosopher Madhava as their new contender.

E: Berkeley is the West's offering, and he is straight in there on the attack. Here he goes, he's making a Profound Statement: 'To be is to be perceived or to perceive.'

MZ: Well, it's a strong start. Although Madhava looks puzzled. I'm not sure he quite knows where Berkeley is going with this argument. He's opening his mouth to make a reply.

E: But Berkeley is in again with yet more philosophy! He's really on fire, is Berkeley. He's not going to let Madhava get a word in edgeways.

MZ: Now I say, I'm not sure that's decent conversational conduct!

E: 'Therefore, if I do not perceive you, you do not exist.' Well that's an interesting line of argument.

MZ: He's turning round – he's refusing to perceive Madhava!

E: And it looks like this duel may be over before it's even begun. By the power of Berkeley's philosophy, Madhava is ceasing to exist! Without even being able to get a word in his defence!

MZ: I can't believe this is it for Hindu philosophy! The Eastern side are furious, the Western side are celebrating their victory already. And it really does look like it's a done deal.

E: Another point for the West.

MZ: Wait a second… I don't believe it! Madhava is reincarnating! And that's a huge sigh of relief from the East. It looks like he's back in the game.

E: Berkeley is flabbergasted, and Madhava is speaking.

MZ: Finally!

E: He says… 'Does a table in an empty room disappear, only to reappear when someone comes in and thus perceives it?'

MZ: A good response.

E: He does look smug about that come-back.

MZ: And well he might, by continuing to exist after Berkeley refused to perceive him has effectively destroyed Berkeley's philosophy.

E: I always did find Berkeley's theories rather flawed.

MZ: Madhava is already continuing... 'Enlightenment can only be achieved through absence from all desire. I have no desires.'

E: Umm... interesting. Here's Berkeley's response: 'Do you not desire to win?'

MZ: Madhava: 'No, since defeating your philosophy I no longer have need of the desire to win.'

E: Well – it seems Berkeley is in a tough spot here now. His philosophy hasn't worked, so he is weapon-less, and Madhava is in the process of proving that he has achieved Enlightenment.

MZ: I think it may be another victory for the East... Berkeley is turning round so that he may refuse to perceive his opponent. Although it's a token effort, he must already have realised that can't work – Madhava will just reincarnate!

E: The crowd is hushed awaiting Madhava's reincarnation...

MZ: ... I think Madhava may have shot himself in the foot by declaring himself free from desires...

E: Really?

MZ: Yes, he didn't mention that through the absence of desire and the attaining of Enlightenment you are liberated from the rebirth process. I don't think he was banking on Berkeley trying his method again!

E: A philosophical own-goal?

MZ: Just that!

E: Well it doesn't look as though Madhava is going to reincarnate – so it's another victory for the West! This is nail-biting stuff.

Round 4: Berkeley vs. Buddha

MZ: The East are now presenting… Buddha. Berkeley rubs his hands together in readiness.

E: He's straight in there with the not-perceiving of Buddha.

MZ: Buddha's speaking: 'I am perceived by God, who perceives everything.'

E: Well!

MZ: Berkeley looks rather shocked. He's speaking… 'But you don't believe in God!'

E: 'Yes I do!' Buddha is retorting. And who's to argue with that?

MZ: And as Buddha claims he is perceived by God, of course Berkeley's method doesn't work. Whether or not Buddha is telling the truth, of course, is unknown – however it is not the place of the casual bystander to challenge the beliefs of history's greatest thinkers.

E: Buddha is taking the initiative… 'Surely a good sophist is able to win an argument even if they are wrong?' Berkeley hasn't been able to say anything; it's a direct challenge to his silence.

MZ: He's continuing: 'A true philosopher, regardless of opinion, can argue any point of view.'

E: It looks as though he's using Western philosophy against him. An unusual tactic to be sure.

MZ: Hmmm... Berkeley has no response. He's trying the not-perceiving tactic one last time, but I believe his luck has run out. Buddha is the winner! And without really using any Buddhist philosophy. Is that permitted in the rules?

E: Well it must be, they're allowing it!

Round 5: Buddha vs. Descartes

MZ: Next up is Descartes.

E: He's embarking on a method of logical doubt. This should be interesting… he's philosophising hard.

MZ: Ahh, he's going back to the old favourite – 'Je pense, donc je suis!'

E: In English, please.

MZ: 'I think, therefore I am!'

E: Well there's a philosophical cliché if ever I heard one. I'm not quite sure where he's going with that argument.

MZ: Yes, I think he's rather used to being able to impress anyone with that. Buddha does not look so impressed. 'Your philosophy is based on the questions of existence, and the importance of your own existence?'

E: Descartes is responding: 'Yes, my own existence is the only certainty. I am not even sure that you exist – you could just be a trick of my own mind.'

MZ: Looks like he's trying to follow the same route that Thales and Berkeley took. Buddha's continuing: 'The idea of Self is the root of all suffering.'

E: Gosh! Nice move.

MZ: He's going on again: 'The aim of my practice is to end the stress of existence.'

E: But Descartes' philosophy depends on existence… a bit of a stalemate here, whose is going to end up the more powerful?

MZ: Buddha is speaking again: 'If I were to, say, do you a favour and end your existence, how would you know it was me doing the ending, and not your mind doing it to you?'

E: Descartes is giving the question due consideration – 'I wouldn't, I would have to assume that your existence was unlikely and that the cause of this end of my existence was in my own head.'

MZ: Descartes seems to be puzzling over the possibility of causing the end of his own existence with his own thoughts. He's saying, 'And in that case, if I am prone to cause my own existence to end with my own thoughts then, in the interest of self-preservation, I'd better not think at all.'

E: Ah! I see what Buddha's done! He's caused Descartes to stop thinking, and thus cause his own inexistence as his thoughts are the only things which prove that he does, in fact, exist.

MZ: And there we have the end of the match! Very smoothly done. Is there no-one who can defeat Buddha?

Round 6: Buddha vs. Protagoras

E: Next to challenge Buddha then – it's Protagoras.

MZ: Here Buddha goes – 'The key to attaining Enlightenment lies in four Noble Truths.'

E: A promising start. This man really does have philosophical stamina. The hopes of the entire Western team lie on Protagoras, if they're to equalise with the East. And Protagoras is straight in there with some philosophy.

MZ: He's saying: 'Truth is merely a matter of opinion.'

E: Well that just about sums up his philosophy in one phrase, and crushes Buddha's.

MZ: I don't believe it! The judges have declared that a win!

E: Well that's the shortest duel so far!

MZ: Surely that can't be right? How can he have won?

E: You cannot argue with the ref!

MZ: I demand a replay!

E: We're meant to be impartial here.

MZ: But I call that decision decisively dodgy…

E: An update on the scores then! It's 3 – all. A close one, it really is.

Round 7: Protagoras vs. Bodhidharma

MZ: Bodhidharma is entering the arena as the next contender for the East.

E: What's his philosophy again?

MZ: Zen Buddhism.

E: Ah, this should be interesting.

MZ: Now, we all know that Western philosophers tend to get confused within their own phraseology and logic, and Zen Buddhism has a very sneaky method of using methods of confusion to confound the conscious mind in order to reach Enlightenment. Unfortunately for a sophist, the moment he himself is confused and no longer coherent, he is lost. Let's see how Bodhidharma will use this against Protagoras...

E: Of course, whereas a Zen Buddhist would reach Enlightenment through confusion, the sophist simply overheats. Protagoras starts with his 'man is the measure of all things' saying.

MZ: Bodhidharma's reaction to that is to take his saying and rearrange it in a confusing manner so that he may meditate upon it.

E: Protagoras looks puzzled, whilst Bodhidharma appears more and more calm.

MZ: And there we have it! Protagoras has argued himself into a state of utter confusion... thus rendering himself impotent. Bodhidharma looks smug, and well he should. He is now having a brief moment of meditation while he awaits his next opponent.

Round 8: Bodhidharma vs. Winnie-the-Pooh

E: There's a flare of trumpets – that means the West are producing their wild-card, their secret weapon. The crowd is hushed, a cloaked figure has stepped into the arena. Every breath is caught as they wait for the surprise contestant to reveal him(or indeed her)self.

MZ: The cloak is whipped off…

E: It's Winnie-the-Pooh!

MZ: Isn't he a character from a children's book?

E: Yes, but if you analyse the book more carefully, it has been said that Pooh encompasses the entirety of Western philosophy. A shrewd move by the West.

MZ: The Bear speaks: 'You can't stay in your corner of the Forest waiting for others to come to you. You have to go to them sometimes.'

E: Unfortunately that has been a cornerstone of Bodhidharma's tactics up till now…

MZ: He's preparing a response, ah, he's using the method of confusion to confound the conscious mind again.

E: 'It is more fun to talk with someone who doesn't use long, difficult words but rather short, easy words like "what about lunch?",' says Pooh.

MZ: Bodhidharma looks puzzled. He's trying a different tactic, this is his method of posing unanswerable questions to meditate upon: 'What was your face like before you were conceived?' Now this form of questioning is designed to empty the conscious mind, again.

E: Well, Pooh's mind is empty already. Here's his response: 'I am a Bear of Very Little Brain, and long words Bother me.' Pooh's not giving in to any of Bodhidharma's attacks, this looks like it's going to be a long battle...

... an hour later...

E: Finally! An end to the tedium! After much heckling from the crowd Bodhidharma is conceding defeat. He's not been able to make any headway against the Bear, and he doesn't really believe in conflict anyway.

MZ: Stay and fight, you pussy! Stay and fight!

E: The East are not pleased, but Bodhidharma has seen that he cannot win this.

MZ: Zen Buddhists are a bunch of fannies.

E: Language, Mao. This is a live broadcast. Bodhidharma is leaving the stadium to the booing of the crowd. Winnie-the-Pooh just looks genially bemused.

MZ: That wasn't a proper feat of philosophy….

Round 9: Winnie-the-Pooh vs. Confucius

E: Well this truly is getting very tense. The West have used up their secret weapon… it's now time for the East to produce theirs… Blare of trumpets…

MZ: Well, of course it has to be Confucius – I'm surprised they've got this far without playing that card really. How's Winnie-the-Pooh going to handle this one?

E: Surely Confucius doesn't stand a chance against the embodiment of Western philosophy? That Bear has Stamina.

MZ: This battle may only go to show how Western philosophy, in the end, is ineffective in comparison to the East.

E: Have we just given up on impartiality completely now, Mao?

MZ: Yes we have. Confucius is preparing himself… this man didn't found China's biggest religion for nothing…

E: I've still got my money on Winnie. There's a lot of substance in that little head of his.

MZ: I thought the point was that there was just a lot of grey fluff?

E: Perhaps, but the point is he's built himself up strong, and it's going to take a lot to beat him. Ah yes, he's preparing to philosophise…

MZ: As is Confucius. He's more than ready to take on the Bear. Winnie-the-Pooh has made the first attack, but Confucius is remaining calm…

E: And, well, oh my… Confucius is now applying his philosophy to a martial art!

And Winnie-the-Pooh just doesn't know where to look. Winnie-the-Pooh has taken a blow. It's not looking good… Confucius is just too fast for him.

MZ: Well, I'm not sure how he can win this now, you can never defeat a Kung Fu Master.

E: … He's thinking deeply… is he going to pronounce a Profound Thought, to sweep Confucius away?

MZ: Is that a pot of honey in his hands?

E: He's putting it on the ground in front of him – the crowd is hushed, awaiting his words.

MZ: He's spoken.

E: 'Tut tut, it looks like rain.'

MZ: And so it does.

The match is called off due to rain: the philosophers troop inside for tea and cucumber sandwiches.

E: Well! What a climax!

CHAPTER 7

How to Become a Philosopher

'One can only become a philosopher, but not be one. As one believes he is a philosopher, he stops being one'
Friedrich Von Schlegel

Everybody who likes to think of themselves as having Deep Thoughts would secretly like to be considered a philosopher. Here is an easy guide to fulfilling this desire. Follow the steps carefully and you cannot go wrong.

1. Learn about Maths. Most (Western) philosophers seem to have been mathematicians at some point. Plato himself had written over the door of his Academy 'Let no-one ignorant of Mathematics enter here'. It couldn't hurt to get off to a good start.

2. Develop a philosophy, preferably somewhere very barren, remote, and intellectual (to reflect the nature of most other philosophies). While creating your philosophy you should bear the following in mind:

☯ First, find yourself some –isms to associate yourself with, which you can later branch away from and claim you never had anything to do with in the first place

- Find yourself a good strong metaphor – often there is little difference between philosophies except for the metaphors used to explain them

- Take an inventive stand on religion – controversial religious beliefs used to get a philosopher into trouble, but now are an essential element in any modern philosophy

☯ To give your philosophy a bit of zest, make an outrageous statement that no-one else will be able to compete with. This is a good way to grab attention and win that extra bit of publicity needed to get a young philosophy off the ground

☯ Ask the question 'why?' about everything. And then ask 'why?' about every conclusion you have reached. This is a really good way to be abstract and get good confusing and convoluted claims

❂ Don't discriminate with what you think up – include it all in your philosophy. Even bad ideas can be argued to be good ones in philosophy

❂ Try to make all your Thoughts open-ended. This way if someone criticises you, you can always claim you meant something else. This is also a good way of making your philosophy universal – everyone will be able to interpret it in a way that suits them!

❂ Come up with a good meaning of life – they're always fun and may get you more followers as everyone wants to know the answer to this

☯ Make a load of spurious claims that you can't prove, but nobody else can disprove. This will encourage people to Think More Deeply about your philosophy

☯ Use random capital letters, it makes it look like what you write is Important Terminology

☯ Use an interesting method of presenting your philosophy – for example, Plato used dialogues involving his hero, Socrates, and other Greeks

● Think up a catchy name for your philosophy – check to see if your own name sounds good with '- ism' at the end of it. If it doesn't, translate the main point of your philosophy into Ancient Greek or Latin

● Think of some quotable lines – like literary sound-bites, or 'philo-bites', as we shall call them

● Check on Google (the Source of All Knowledge) to make sure no-one else has already invented your philosophy

3. Tell others about your philosophy – a philosophy is useless unless it is inflicted on innocent bystanders.

4. Collect a cult of followers. Enlisting a group of students is a good way to do this. Students will do anything if they think it will make them look intellectual.

5. Establish yourself as an Intellectual. Back this up by writing a book or paper on your philosophy – the most important thing here is to be published.

6. Perform a couple of good publicity stunts to get your philosophy noticed by the wider population and to entice more followers.

7. Die for your cause and immortalise your philosophy (optional).

CHAPTER 8

Case Study: Vestiariumism

Now, as I myself may be occasionally guilty of pretensions to Deep Thoughts, following the foolproof guide I outlined in the previous chapter I shall now become a Philosopher.

Step 1: Learn About Maths

Well this should be easy, I got a GCSE in Maths, I should be fine on that count. And I can cash-up a till at the end of the day – the only practical Maths you'll ever need.

Step 2: Develop a Philosophy

I chose Arthur's Seat in Edinburgh to be my remote place, and hid behind a rock so that I could pretend that the runners who sporadically went past me weren't there. I felt very Alone and Intellectual.

☯ For my inspirational (and later discarded) –isms I consulted Wikipedia and chose:

Cartesianism – The only thing you can prove exists is the thinking self, e.g. 'I know as the sole existent in this universe that my welfare is more important than non-existent work for some non-existent boss. If nothing exists beyond my mind, how can I have work to do?'

Anthropomorphism – The attribution of human characteristics to non-human things, e.g. 'That cloud looks like a man with a headache. This proves that clouds have feelings that should not be dismissed.'

Antinomianism – Members of particular religious groups are not obliged to follow the laws of ethics or morality as set down by religious authorities, i.e. 'God is flawless and without imperfection, so has no need of bathing. Therefore I don't need to either.'

Immortalism – The belief in existing for an infinite length of time, e.g. 'If you look at it in context, then we all exist eternally and in the long run this bit of time is only fleeting anyway, so I'm not really late at all.'

Nihilism – Here, human existence and the world in general is purposeless, meaningless, without truth or value, as has been said: 'suicide is painless, it brings so many changes and you can take or leave it if you please'.

Expressionism – The distortion of reality for added emotional effect: 'I didn't break it! I instilled it with the essence of… love!'

- ☯ **Metaphor**: Life is a wardrobe with a back that opens up and leads to Narnia.

- ☯ **Religious theory**: God is a mothball who lives in my old shoe.

- ☯ **Outrageous statement**: You are not obliged to follow the laws of ethics or morality as set down by society, as they are a bunch of squares, and triangles are the truth in reality.

- ☯ **Meaning of life**: To reach Narnia, and to find the elusive Lost Trainer.

A dialogue between Sherlock Holmes (a fictional detective) and Baldrick (a fictional fool):

SHERLOCK HOLMES: The only thing that you can prove exists is your thinking mind. The existence of this mind is pointless and without value. The thinking mind is a vast wardrobe.

BALDRICK: If the only thing that exists is your thinking mind, how did your thinking mind come to exist?

HOLMES: It has always existed and always will.

BALDRICK: Like God?

HOLMES: God is a mothball that lives in the old shoe in my Wardrobe. He (or She) aims to eliminate the moths that eat my clothes. The moths are the sinners that decay the Wardrobe.

BALDRICK: How can there be sinners? I thought it was only your thinking mind that exists?

HOLMES: Yes, I mean the sinners that I imagine. The Wardrobe is immortal, for it cannot end.

BALDRICK: Unless it is burnt.

HOLMES: The Wardrobe as a concept exists infinitely. Whether is it burnt or not is inconsequential. It cannot be burnt down because that would imply that there is someone or something outside the Wardrobe to burn it. And it cannot be burnt from the inside because there are no matches.

BALDRICK: What if you have a wardrobe with matches?

HOLMES: Such a person would be self-destructive, in fact, they don't exist, as the only thinking mind that exists is my own and I don't keep matches in my Wardrobe. The concept of matches is alien to a Wardrobe interior. Therefore, as the Wardrobe cannot be burnt except from the inside where you cannot get matches, the soul cannot die and is immortal.

BALDRICK: Isn't it murder, destroying metaphorical moths?

HOLMES: I do not believe in the need to follow the laws of ethics or morality as set down by society. For they are all in my own mind, and one does not always need to do exactly what your own mind tells you, otherwise there would be no will power. The meaning of life–

BALDRICK: I thought you said life was meaningless?

HOLMES: No, I said that existence is meaningless. Life is not meaningless. The meaning of life is to reach Narnia. We can only reach Narnia once we have found the Lost Trainer and mended the moth-eaten jacket which we are to take to Narnia, which is in the back of the Wardrobe.

BALDRICK: But I thought the wardrobe was infinite – how can it have a back?

HOLMES: Well where would you put Narnia?

BALDRICK: Hang on a minute! If your thinking mind is the only thing you can prove exists, how can you say that there is a God?

HOLMES: God exists in my mind.

BALDRICK: What if you were to come out of your closet?

HOLMES: Well that would be the end of life as we know it, Baldrick.

BALDRICK: What a ridiculous philosophy, if you can call it a philosophy at all.

HOLMES: Philosophy is just words.

BALDRICK: No, philosophy is thought.

HOLMES: No, thought is thought and philosophy is words used to confuse thought...

The Name: I decided immediately that 'Hathawayism' did not look or sound any good. The most obvious after this was of course 'Narnianwardrobeism' (based on the principle theories behind my philosophy) – but this has far too many syllables to be a credible philosophy – no intellectual would be seen dead spending more time pronouncing their musings than musing. It is also so easy to understand that mere mortals would be able to understand the philosophy from its name, and this would simply not do. The solution? Latin of course! My Pocket Latin Dictionary told me the word for wardrobe is 'vestiarium'. 'Vestiariumism' not only sounds cool, but will be tricky for someone to pronounce first time. Correcting lesser mortals is the first step to true intellect. The number of syllables is on the excessive side, but I knew that the philosophy itself was strong enough to be taken seriously on merit of content alone.

Cool philo-bites: 'Existence is meaningless, but life is not', 'No matches, God is extremely flammable', 'What's in YOUR wardrobe?', 'The only way to true enlightenment is through Narnia'.

When my own philosophy was at last complete, I did a quick Google search for 'Vestiariumism', which told me that no-one else had yet invented it. I was ready to present it to the world.

Step 3: Inflict Your Philosophy on Others

To do this I took the classic stand of getting drunk and, sounding oh-so-clever, tried to impress my social peers with it at a house party. Enlisting the enthusiasm of none of them, I preached it outside of Edinburgh University main library (a standard place for people to inflict their views on others) in the form of flyers and a cake stall. I was justly ignored, as is customary for people who adopt this method, although the chocolate rice-crispy cakes sold well. Feeling the need to branch out, I also made a day-trip to St. Andrews University, realising that pretension levels there might be higher than at Edinburgh and I might have more luck. There I found a coffee shop (everyone knows that philosophers either drink or muse in coffee shops using the smallest cups they can possibly find to drink out of) and proclaimed from the tabletop to the unwary masses that God is a small white sphere of pest control that lives in my shoe.

Step 4: Collect a Cult of Followers

On my search for a student following I toured as many student societies as I could, peddling my philosophy. I was barred from all until I happened upon a meeting for the Edinburgh University Scottish Ethnology Society and presented to them my philosophy. They were immediately converted and with much enthusiasm became the first Vestiariumists. There was one dissenter, but he was silenced and immediately broke away to form a rebel branch of the Scottish Ethnology Society, the Ethnology of Scotland Society (splitter!). I also started up a 'Vestiariumism' group on Facebook (the ultimate internet stalking engine), which was popular with procrastinators of all shapes and sizes.

Step 5: Establish Yourself as an Intellectual

I cemented the importance and credibility of my philosophy through publication – this publication, to be precise – therefore ensuring that my words cannot be doubted.

Step 6: Perform a Couple of Publicity Stunts

The Scottish Ethnology Society (but not the Ethnology of Scotland Society) was very eager to help me draw further attention to Vestiariumism. They then suggested holding a ceilidh in its honour, however it was decided that this was not Radical enough for such an important philosophy. In the end nude carol singing was decided upon, although the extreme Edinburgh cold made the duration of the performance brief. And public nudity laws meant that we had to wrap ourselves in a banner adorned with the slogan 'Vestiariumism, you know it makes sense'. A hearty rendition of 'God rest ye merry Vestiariumists' went down a treat.

The newspaper reports of the event are archived at the School of Scottish Studies, University of Edinburgh.

Step 7: Die for Your Cause

Obviously I was unwilling to actually die myself, as I do not know how the world would cope without me. In a feat of selflessness I decided that it would be prudent to sacrifice my pseudonym 'Dan Vice' on the altar of intellect, and therefore caused Dan to die in a tragic bungee-jumping episode whilst declaring the main theories of Vestiariumism. Thus immortalised, Vestiariumism is now a true Philosophy, and myself a true Philosopher.

CHAPTER 9

The Great
Philosophical Jokes
of Our Time

Q: How many philosophers does it take to change a light bulb?

A: Depends on how you define 'change'.

A: How can you be sure it needs changing?

A: Three. One to change it and two to stand around arguing whether or not the light bulb exists.

Q: How many natural selectionists does it take to change a light bulb?

A: None, they won't actually try to change the light bulb, but simply stop using the room containing the burnt-out bulb, and start only using rooms with functioning bulbs. That way, over time…

Q: How many Epicureans does it take to change a light bulb?

A: None – they're too busy taking advantage of the darkness!

Q: How many existentialists does it take to change a light bulb?

A: Two. One to change the light bulb and one to observe how the light bulb symbolises an incandescent beacon of subjectivity in a netherworld of Cosmic Nothingness.

Q: How many Marxists does it take to change a light bulb?

A: None. The light bulb contains the seeds of its own revolution.

Q: How many Episcopalians does it take to change a light bulb?

A: Six. One to change the bulb, and five to form a society to preserve the memory of the old light bulb.

Q: How many Zen masters does it take to change a light bulb?

A: Two. One to change it, and one not to change it.

A: Three. One to change it, one not to change it, and one both to change it and not to change it.

Q: How many Hegelians does it take to change a light bulb?

A: Two, of course. One stands at one end of the room and argues that it isn't dark; the other stands at the other end and says that true light is impossible. This dialogue creates a synthesis which does the job.

Q: How many surrealists does it take to change a light bulb?

A: Two. One to change the elephant and one to fill the bath with multicoloured power tools.

Q: Why did the chicken cross the road?

A: **Epicurus**: For fun.

A: **Einstein**: Whether the chicken crossed the road or the road crossed the chicken depends upon your frame of reference.

A: **Zeno**: To prove it could never reach the other side.

A: **Plato**: For the greater good.

A: **Nietzsche**: Because if you gaze too long across the Road, the Road also gazes across you.

A: **Descartes**: Since the chicken does not really exist it was only an illusion that the chicken crossed the road. This illusion was only in my mind. Therefore I created the chicken that crossed the road.

A: **Darwin**: It was the logical next step after coming down from the trees.

A: **Sphinx**: You tell me.

A: **George W. Bush**: We don't really care why the chicken crossed the road. We just want to know whether the chicken is on our side of the road or not. The chicken is either with us or against us. There is no middle ground here.

A: **Bill Gates**: I have just released eChicken 2007, which will not only cross roads, but will lay eggs, file your important documents, and balance your cheque-book.

A: **Dr. Seuss**: Did the chicken cross the road? Did he cross it with a toad? Yes, the chicken crossed the road, but why it crossed, I've not been told!

A: **Hemingway**: To die. In the rain. Alone.

A: **Marx**: It was a historical inevitability.

A: **Freud**: Was it a chicken or a cock you saw crossing the road?

A: **Douglas Adams**: Forty-two.

Q: What did the Buddhist say to the hot-dog seller?

A: Make me one with everything.

Q: What did the hot-dog seller say when the Buddhist asked for his change?

A: Change comes from within.

Q: What's the difference between a philosopher and a doctor?

A: About £50,000 a year.

Q: What do you get when you cross the Godfather with a philosopher?

A: An offer you can't understand.

Q: How do you get a philosopher off your doorstep?

A: Pay for the pizza.

Q: What do you get if you cross an insomniac, agnostic and a dyslexic?

A: Someone who stays awake all night wondering if there really is a Dog.

'To do is to be' – Kant
'To be is to do' – Nietzsche
'Do be do be do' – Frank Sinatra

'A philosopher,' said the theologian, 'is like a blind man in a darkened room looking for a black cat that isn't there.'
'That's right,' said the philosopher, 'if he were a theologian he'd find it.'

The First Law of Philosophy: For every philosopher, there exists an equal and opposite philosopher.
The Second Law of Philosophy: They're both wrong.

Descartes is sitting in a bar, having a drink. The bartender asks him if he would like another. 'I think not,' he says and vanishes in a puff of logic.

A sensual guide to academic departments:
Don't LOOK at anything in a physics lab
Don't TASTE anything in a chemistry lab
Don't SMELL anything in a biology lab
Don't TOUCH anything in a medical lab
And most importantly…
Don't LISTEN to anything in a philosophy department.

Jean-Paul Sartre is sitting in a French café, revising his draft of Being and Nothingness. He says to the waitress, 'I'd like a cup of coffee, please, with no cream.' The waitress replies, 'I'm sorry, monsieur, but we're out of cream. How about with no milk?'

www.crombiejardine.com